Dewdrops on the Honeybee

Anita Powell

Presentation by *BookLeaf Publishing*

Web: www.bookleafpub.com

E-mail: info@bookleafpub.com

ISBN: 9789357213004

First edition 2023

This book is dedicated to you. To each and every person who experienced something traumatizing and thought that would be the end. To each and every person who is scared to tell their story. To each and every person who wants to give up. To each and every person who doesn't yet see the light at the end of the tunnel.

I've been there and I promise... It does get better!

ACKNOWLEDGEMENT

This endeavor would not have been possible without Book Leaf Publishing, as they finally pulled me out of my comfort zone and allowed me this platform to reach other survivors like myself.

PREFACE

I saw this poem challenge and thought it would be a great first step on my journey of becoming a motivational speaker. What I didn't realize is how many others have been through similar experiences and did not end at the same place. My hope is that everyone that reads this book will take it to heart and not give up before they get to their rainbow.

Hello

He lied.
She cried.
The baby is gone.

So many punches.
Kicking and screaming.
What happens next?
We all know.

Blackened eyes.
Bleeding nose.
He's got a knife to her throat.

Then one day it ends,
The sun comes out.
She can breathe again.

All that is left is her
sun kissed skin.
All of those scars
glistening from within.

She is free.
She is me.
Me is free.

-Anita Devi

Beauty

I don't like what I see in the mirror.
I don't know that person.
Has everything always been saggy?
Will I forever wear clothes that are baggy?

I don't like what I see in the mirror.
I pinch and grab and poke.
Has my stomach always been soupy?
Will my body keep getting droopy?

I don't like what I see in the mirror.
I've changed so much over the years.
Has that part always been flappy?
Will I ever be happy?

I don't like what I see in the mirror.
I feel like a different species.
Has my smile always been frumpy?
Will my ass forever feel dumpy?

Clockwork

I open my eyes
Like clockwork.
I brush my teeth
Like clockwork.
I shower and dress
Like clockwork.
I breathe and reflect
Like clockwork.

I breathe and reflect
Like clockwork.
I shower and dress
Like clockwork.
I brush my teeth
Like clockwork.
I close my eyes
Like clockwork.

Again

You can breathe again, if you try
Don't let him win, not that guy.

Heal your heart, cry your tears
But don't give in to all your fears

Hurt

5

You hurt yourself to hide the pain but what good
does that do?
Does it take the pain away or put it somewhere
new?
You say it helps distract your mind but we know
that's not true.
When it's all said and done you'll end up black
and blue.

Window

Out my window
I see cars driving by,
People running fast,
A bird flying high.

Out my window
I see clouds so grey,
Buildings made of brick,
A wife begging him to stay.

Out my window
I see glowing lights up,
Snowmen in the yard,
A holiday Starbucks cup.

Out my window
I see bikes out for sale,
Couches block the sidewalks,
A shovel and a pale.

Out my window
I see happy children grow,
Dogs running around
A mother full of woe.

Lost

Some days I feel so lost
Like I am sinking and drowning
With no air in sight.

Some days I feel so whole
Like I am shining and flying
With no limit in sight.

Girl

I wish I knew the power within,
Buried deep under my skin.
A ray of sunshine on my face,
The wind showed me to float with grace.

We have come from the Earth;
Why don't we see what we're worth?

Our cycle syncs with the moon,
Our blood flows to her tune.
Our legs grow long and thick like trees,
We taste like honey from the bees.

Winter

Lights shining so bright
What a beautiful sight.
Kids decorating the tree
A big mug of egg nog for me.
Puppies snuggled nice and warm
Wind howling like a storm.
Presents wrapped so very neat
I'm settling in with a treat.

Healing

"Healing isn't easy"
No one said it was.
It's a lot of hard work
Even when things feel hopeless.
You still stand up and fight your demons
And pray that it will get better someday.

Dim

No matter how dark and dim it feels,
One day the sun will shine again
And it will warm you to the core.

Yes

You can heal.
You can heal.
You can heal.
Even when it feels like you are too broken.
You can cleanse.
You can cleanse.
You can cleanse.
Even when it feels like you are too negative.
You can grow.
You can grow.
You can grow.
Even when it feels like you are too stuck.
You can learn.
You can learn.
You can learn.
Even when it feels like you are forgetting.
You can glow.
You can glow.
You can glow.
Even when it feels like you are dull.

Snowglobe

I look at this snowglobe and feel like I'm home.
A little toy snowman trapped in a dome.
It gets turned and shaken
I feel my heart breakin'
The glittering snow glistening below.
Shining and shimmering the wind starts to blow.

Magic

Feel the magic flow.
Close your eyes
Start to glow.
Think about what you want
And where you would like to go.
Look in the mirror
Do you know,
You are just
Beginning to grow.

Inspired

Because of you I learned to live.
We love exploring
What the world could give.

You taught me how to be a mom.
Even though the first diaper
Felt like diffusing a bomb.

Because of you I never quit.
Even when I'm battered
And feel like shit.

You taught me how to love so deep.
How peaceful it is
To watch you sleep.

Because of you I grew and grew.
We grew together
Because our love is true.

You taught me how to see the light.
You are my sun
That shines so bright.

Happily

From sadness and darkness and trauma within,
I never thought my life would begin.
But here comes a man so tall, dark, and thin,
He offers his love; it feels like a win.

Ever

We travel the world and share every bite,
and passion and heat from every fight.
He lifts me up and holds me tight,
When I look in his eyes, I see love burning
bright.

After

I finally got my happy end
Laughter and giggles are my new trend.
It feels incredible, I'm on the mend,
In my husband I found my best friend.